Carolyn Miller

Student Favorites

Book 2

Notes from the Publisher

Composers in Focus is a series of original piano collections celebrating the creative artistry of contemporary composers. It is through the work of these composers that the piano teaching repertoire is enlarged and enhanced.

It is my hope that students, teachers, and all others who experience this music will be enriched and inspired.

Frank J. Hackinson

Frank J. Hackinson, Publisher

Notes from the Composer

Student Favorites, Book Two contains a variety of moods, ranging from the upbeat Spanish rhythms of *Danza* to the soothing melodies of *Daydreaming*. There is something for everyone in this collection.

It is my hope that students and teachers will want to use these pieces for study as well as performance—and that they will become some of your favorites, too.

Carolyn Miller

Carolyn Miller

Contents

Danza

*Play this piece with a strong sense of rhythm, as though you
were accompanying an exciting Spanish dance.*

Carolyn Miller

With energy and drama (♩ = 92-108)

4

FF1195

Best Friends

This piece should be played with an easy swing.
At measure 25, be sure to bring out the melody in the left hand.

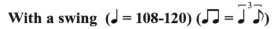

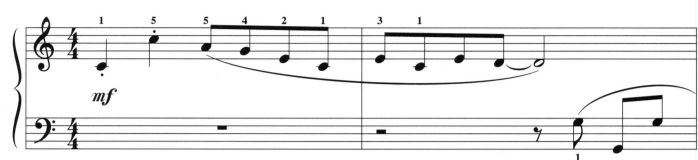

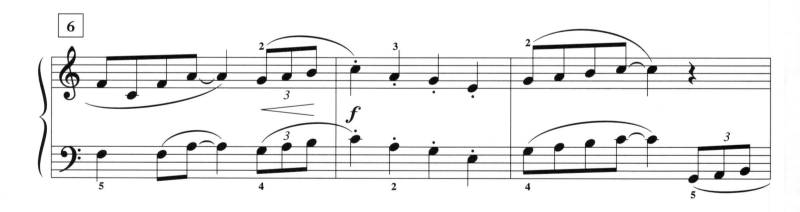

8

Daydreaming

Resting outdoors, looking up at the sky… watching the clouds drifting by…
This piece captures the relaxed mood of a quiet afternoon.

10

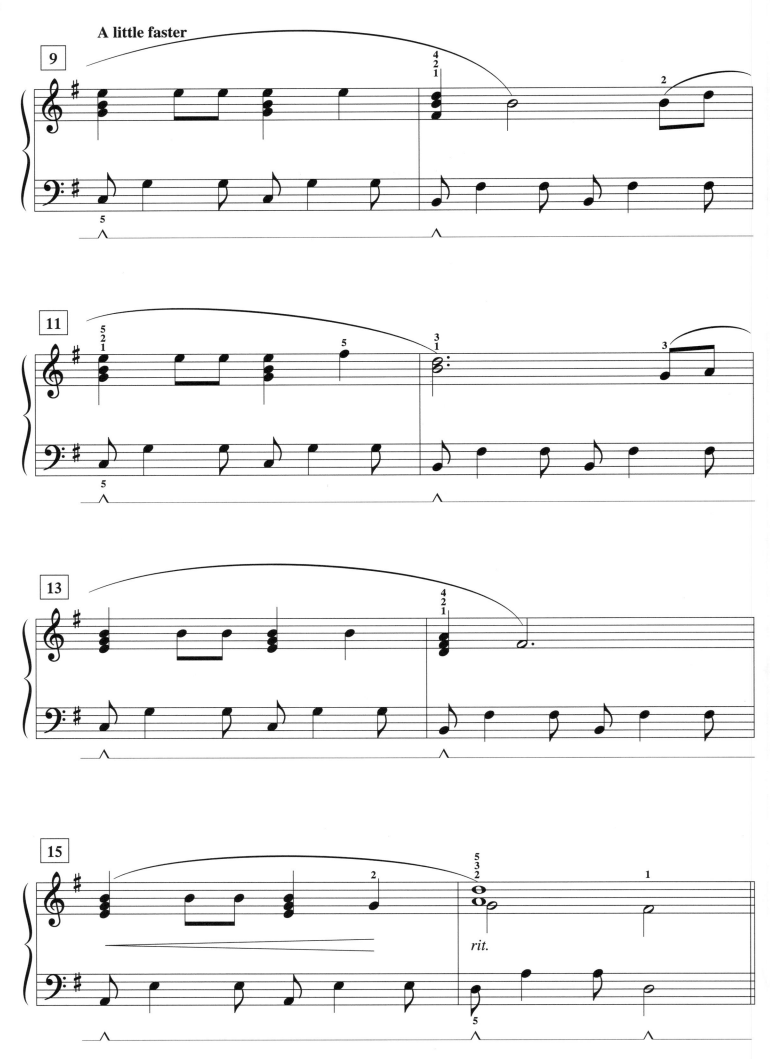

12

Butterfly Dance

This solo should begin with a brilliant, exciting sound. At measure 9, the butterfly
circles around mysteriously before the return of the main theme at measure 25.

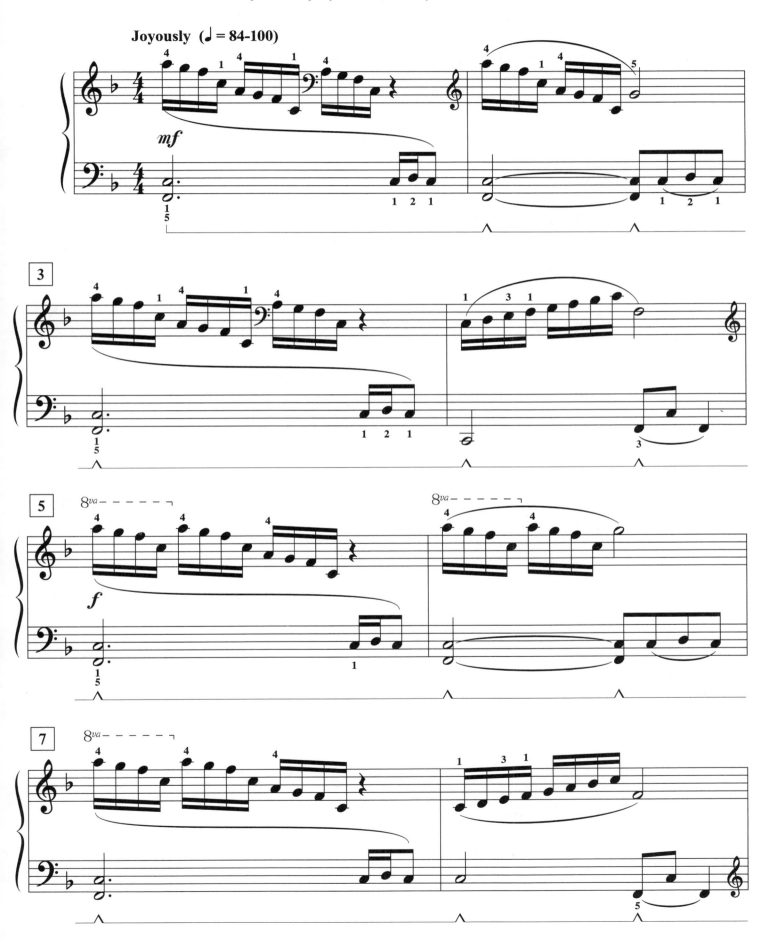

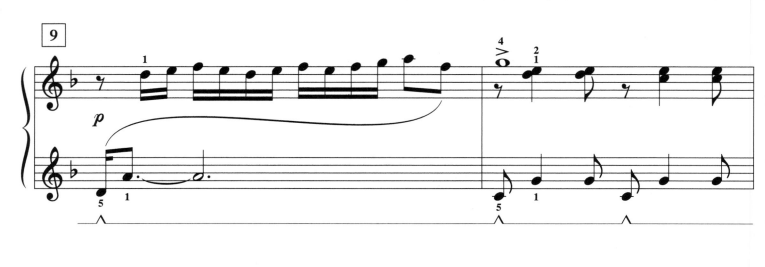

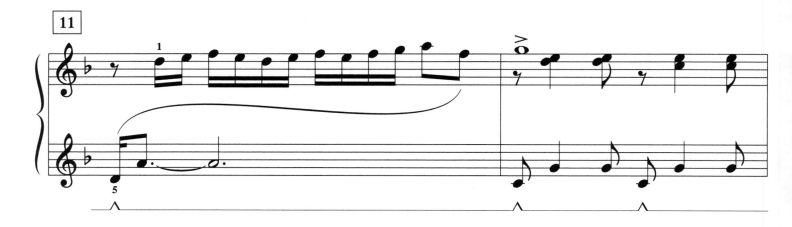

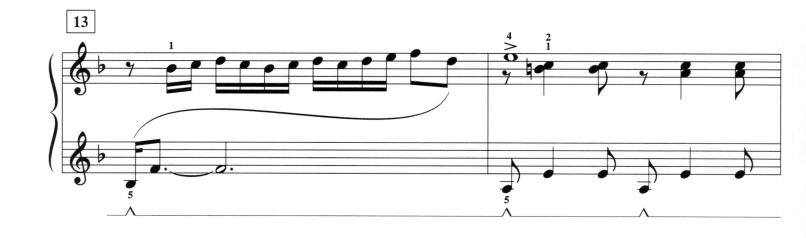

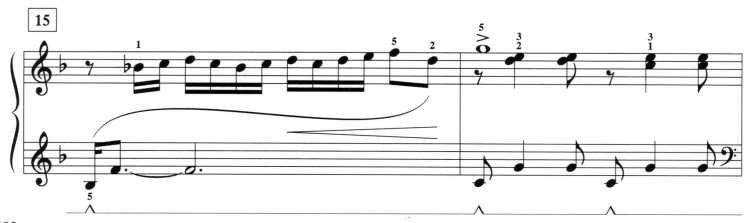

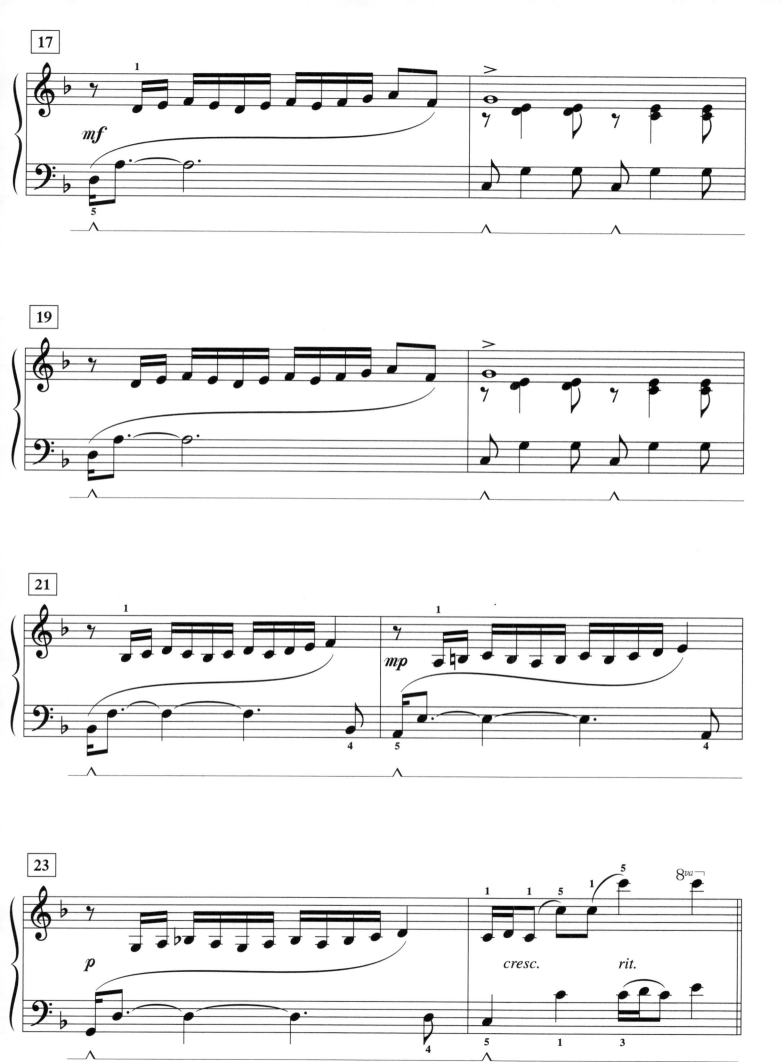

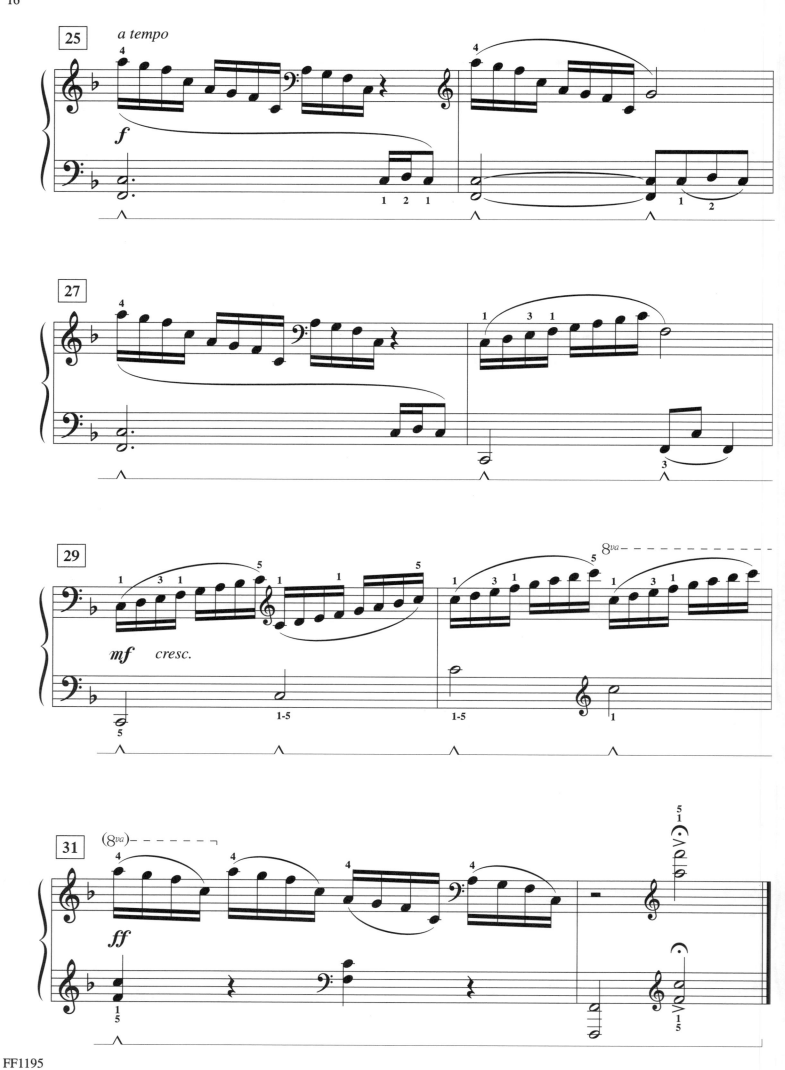

At River Bend

This melody should be played very expressively.
Try to make up a story to fit the music. What does the title suggest to you?

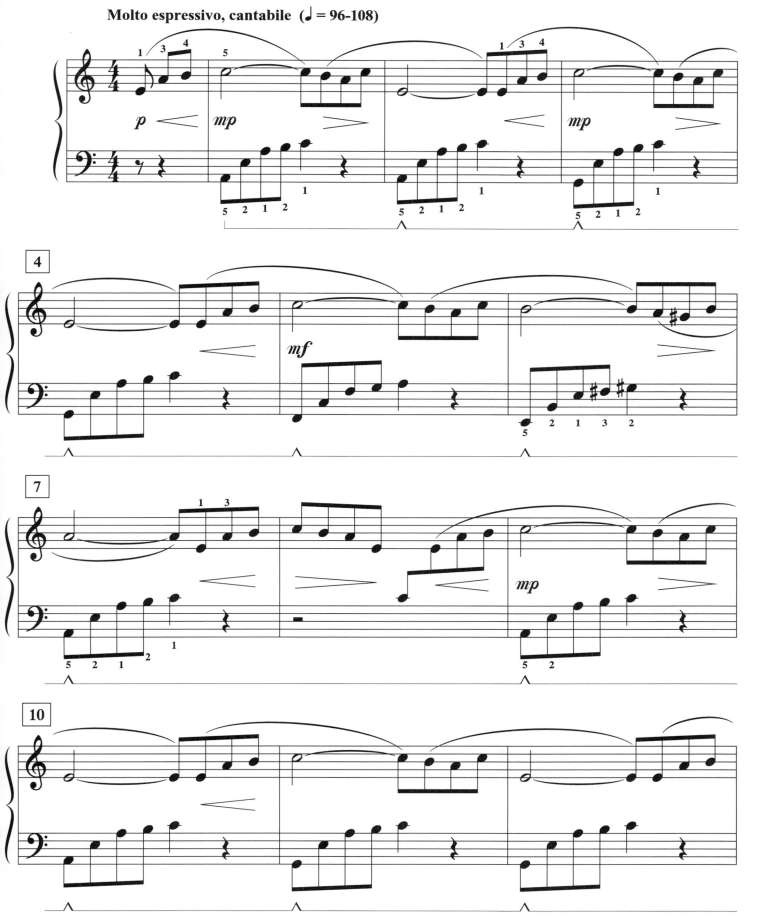

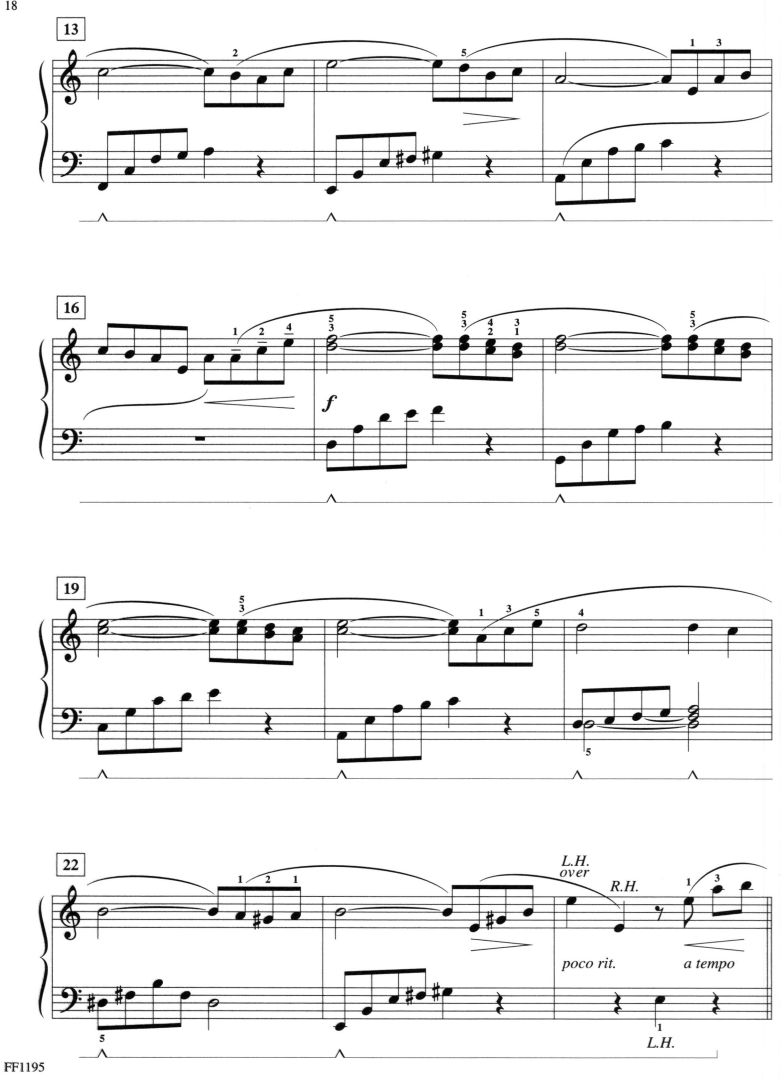

FF1195

Motion Machine

Imagine a "perpetual motion machine" clanking away very precisely.
This piece is built from broken chords; naming the chords makes learning this piece easier.

Fast and precise (♩ = 100-120)

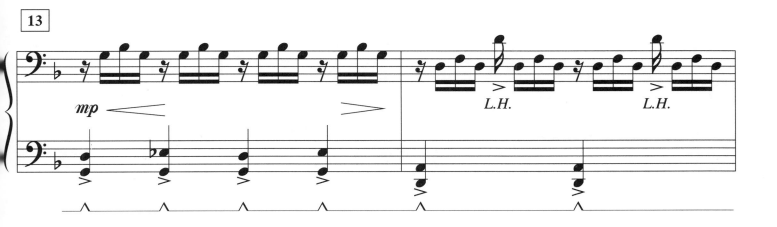

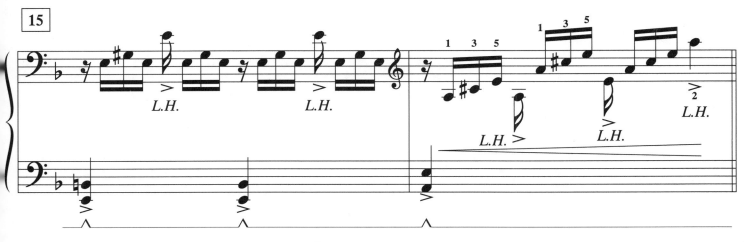